Sports

Soccer
Records

by Paul D. Bowker

FOCUS
READERS®

BEACON

www.focusreaders.com

Focus Readers is distributed by North Star Editions:
sales@northstareditions.com | 888-417-0195

Produced for Focus Readers by Red Line Editorial.

Photographs ©: Pol Emile/Sipa/AP Images, cover, 1; Mo Khursheed/TFV Media/AP Images, 4; Elaine Thompson/AP Images, 7; Tony Gutierrez/AP Images, 8; DB/picture-alliance/dpa/AP Images, 10; Marcio Jose Sanchez/AP Images, 13, 29; Georgios Kefalas/Keystone/AP Images, 14; AP Images, 17; David Vincent/AP Images, 19; Paul Sakuma/AP Images, 20–21; Estadao Conteudo/Agencia Estado/AP Images, 22; Greg Baker/AP Images, 24; Daniel Ochoa De Olza/AP Images, 27

Library of Congress Cataloging-in-Publication Data
Names: Bowker, Paul, 1954- author.
Title: Soccer records / by Paul D. Bowker.
Description: Lake Elmo, MN : Focus Readers, [2021] | Series: Sports records | Includes index. | Audience: Grades 4-6
Identifiers: LCCN 2020005914 (print) | LCCN 2020005915 (ebook) | ISBN 9781644933640 (hardcover) | ISBN 9781644934401 (paperback) | ISBN 9781644935927 (pdf) | ISBN 9781644935163 (ebook)
Subjects: LCSH: Soccer--Records--Juvenile literature.
Classification: LCC GV943.25 .B69 2021 (print) | LCC GV943.25 (ebook) | DDC 796.334--dc23
LC record available at https://lccn.loc.gov/2020005914
LC ebook record available at https://lccn.loc.gov/2020005915

Printed in the United States of America
Mankato, MN
082020

About the Author

Paul D. Bowker is an editor and author who splits his living between Cape Cod, Massachusetts, and Florida. His 35-year newspaper and online writing career has included hundreds of US National Team and college soccer games. He is also a certified club referee for the US Soccer Federation. He is a past national president of Associated Press Sports Editors and has won multiple national writing awards.

Table of Contents

Chapter 1

Lloyd's Hat Trick

Carli Lloyd had already scored twice for Team USA. The ball was at her feet again. She **dribbled** up the field. She kicked the ball long. It sailed over the head of Japan's **goalkeeper**. The ball hit the post.

Carli Lloyd scored six goals during the 2015 Women's World Cup.

Then it bounced into the goal. Lloyd ran down the field and celebrated with her teammates.

Lloyd's goal came in the final of the 2015 Women's **World Cup**. It was her third goal of the game. And it happened in the game's 16th minute. Lloyd broke the record

Fun Fact

Team USA goalkeeper Hope Solo was the first player to have 100 **shutouts** in **international** games.

 Carli Lloyd (10) set a record for fastest goal in a World Cup final. She scored in the third minute.

for fastest **hat trick** in World Cup history. Her goals helped Team USA win its third Women's World Cup title.

Chapter 2

World Cup Records

In 2002, Hakan Sukur scored the quickest goal in World Cup history. His team, Turkey, was playing against South Korea. Sukur scored in only 10.9 seconds. Turkey went on to win the game 3–2.

 Hakan Sukur scored a total of 51 goals for Turkey during his career.

 Just Fontaine scored a hat trick in the 1958 third-place game against West Germany.

Goal Machine

The 1958 World Cup was Just Fontaine's first World Cup. It was also his last. But Fontaine made it memorable. He scored 13 goals in the tournament. He set the record for most goals scored in one World Cup. He averaged more than two goals per game.

Perfect in the Net

Germany's Nadine Angerer was not supposed to play much in the 2007 Women's World Cup. She was the backup goalkeeper.

Nadine Angerer led Germany's team to a Women's World Cup victory in 2007. She blocked six penalty kicks in a row.

But the starting goalie was injured.

The pressure was on Angerer.

And she was perfect. She went

540 minutes without giving up a

goal. That was a new record.

Dramatic Finish

Abby Wambach of the United States

made history in the 2011 Women's

In 2019, Brazil's Formiga became the
first person to play in seven World Cups.
She was 41 years old. She's the oldest
player in Women's World Cup history.

 Abby Wambach (20) was named United States Female Player of the Year six times.

World Cup. She **headed** in a goal in the 122nd minute. It was the latest goal scored in a World Cup game. It came in overtime against Brazil. The goal tied the game. The United States won in a **shootout**.

Chapter 3

Tremendous Teams

As of 2021, Brazil has won five World Cup titles. That is more than any other country. Brazil is also the only team that has played in every World Cup.

 Ronaldinho (left) was one of Brazil's best players of the 2000s.

From 1930 to 2018, Brazil won 73 World Cup games.

Brazil was in the World Cup final in 1958. It was the first time they had made the championship. They were playing Sweden. Four minutes into the game, Sweden scored. But then Brazil scored. And they

Fun Fact

A 1950 World Cup game between Brazil and Uruguay drew a record crowd. The stadium was packed with 199,854 people.

 Vavá (far right) scored Brazil's first goal in the 1958 championship game against Sweden.

kept scoring. Brazil won 5–2. They set the record for most goals scored in a World Cup final.

Winning Women

The United States Women's National Team has been on fire.

The 2019 Women's World Cup was their fourth World Cup win. Alex Morgan was a big goal scorer for the team. She scored five goals in a 2019 game against Thailand. Morgan tied a record for the most goals scored in one game. Michelle Akers of the United States first set the record in 1991.

In the 2019 Women's World Cup final, the United States had a 1–0 lead against the Netherlands. Rose Lavelle scored another goal

 Rose Lavelle was a three-time All-American athlete in college.

to make the score 2–0. It was the

26th US goal of the tournament.

That was another Women's

World Cup record.

International Star

Kristine Lilly grew up playing soccer. In high school, she joined the United States Women's National Team. She was 16 years old when she scored her first international goal. She was the first player, male or female, to reach 200 **caps**. Lilly finished her career with 354 caps. That was an all-time record.

Lilly helped the United States win two Women's World Cups. She also won two gold medals and one silver medal in the Olympic Games. Lilly scored her final goal at the age of 38.

Kristine Lilly played in five Women's World Cups.

Chapter 4

Incredible Careers

Pelé won his first World Cup with Brazil at the age of 17. He went on to win two more. Pelé retired with 1,281 career goals. No player has scored more. Many people believe Pelé was the greatest player ever.

Pelé (right) started playing professional soccer when he was 15 years old.

 In 2019, Marta became the first player, male or female, to score in five World Cups.

Best in the World

Marta grew up in a small town in Brazil. She loved playing soccer. But some people thought girls should not play soccer. Marta didn't care. She kept practicing. Many people believe she is the greatest female soccer player.

Fun Fact

In 2019, Marta scored her 17th World Cup goal. No man or woman has scored more goals at the World Cup.

Marta was named Women's Player of the Year six times. No other player has won it more.

Record Year for Messi

Lionel Messi was just 13 years old when he moved from Argentina to Spain. In 2001, he joined FC Barcelona. Messi became one of the

Fun Fact

Asmir Begovic played goalkeeper for Stoke City, an English team. In 2013, he scored from 100.5 yards (91.9 m) away. It was the longest goal ever.

 Lionel Messi had nine hat tricks in 2012. In one game, he scored five goals.

biggest stars in soccer. He could dribble. He could pass. And most of all, he could score. In 2012, he scored 91 goals. That broke the record for most goals scored in one year.

FOCUS ON
Soccer Records

Write your answers on a separate piece of paper.

1. Write a sentence explaining the main idea of Chapter 1.

2. Who do you think is the best soccer player in history? Why?

3. Which country has played in every World Cup?
   A. Argentina
   B. Brazil
   C. Japan

4. Why do many people think Pelé is the greatest soccer player in history?
   A. He played for Brazil.
   B. He scored the most goals.
   C. He started playing professional soccer when he was 15.

5. What does **sailed** mean in this book?

*She kicked the ball long. It **sailed** over the head of Japan's goalkeeper.*

    A. traveled by water

    B. rolled

    C. flew through the air

6. What does **on fire** mean in this book?

*The United States Women's National Team has been **on fire**. The 2019 Women's World Cup was their fourth World Cup win.*

    A. getting burned

    B. successful

    C. playing badly

Answer key on page 32.

Glossary

caps
Appearances in international games.

dribbled
Used small kicks to keep the ball under control.

goalkeeper
A player who can use his or her hands to keep the ball out of the goal.

hat trick
Three goals scored by one player in a game.

headed
Used one's head to hit a soccer ball.

international
Having to do with many different countries.

shootout
When a tie game is decided by players taking penalty shots.

shutouts
Games in which the goalkeeper allows no goals.

World Cup
A soccer tournament involving many countries that takes place every four years.

To Learn More

BOOKS

Kortemeier, Todd. *Kylian Mbappé: Soccer Star.* Lake Elmo, MN: Focus Readers, 2019.

Kortemeier, Todd. *Total Soccer.* Minneapolis: Abdo Publishing, 2017.

Marthaler, Jon. *US Women's Professional Soccer.* Minneapolis: Abdo Publishing, 2019.

NOTE TO EDUCATORS

Visit **www.focusreaders.com** to find lesson plans, activities, links, and other resources related to this title.

Index

Answer Key: 1. Answers will vary; **2.** Answers will vary; **3.** B; **4.** B; **5.** C; **6.** B